Fugue

Fugue

Alejandro Casas

RESOURCE *Publications* · Eugene, Oregon

FUGUE

Resource Publications
An Imprint of Wipf and Stock Publishers
199 W. 8th Ave., Suite 3
Eugene, OR 97401

www.wipfandstock.com

PAPERBACK ISBN: 978-1-5326-9983-2
HARDCOVER ISBN: 978-1-5326-9984-9
EBOOK ISBN: 978-1-5326-9985-6

Manufactured in the U.S.A.   OCTOBER 14, 2019

Contents

Exposition

Prologue

A sunny afternoon, the wind
Brushes on the leaves of
The high and shapely cut trees.
An old man plays with his

Grandson. Enthusiastically the
Old man pursues the toddler
Around the backyard of a modest
Home. There is a young man
Watching, behind the sliding
Doors. He watches as one rolls
And the other groans. The
Reflection of his face on the
Sliding doors is not clear.

Only his light eyes are seen,
Observantly sucking the
Moment to the fullest detail.

The young man is afflicted, he
Feels overwhelmed. Not sure
Why, just that he is drowning
By the weight of his thoughts.

His lungs are filled to the
Top and do not let the air
Pass. He feels as if he does not

Know what the cause is. Just
A simple feeling of perplexity
At his own mind. He has tried

Everything, sports, painting, sex,
Drugs, love, and everything just
Makes him drown even more.

The young man ignores the
Feeling. This works for a
While, then haunts him in
His sleep. What is this?

He claims in despair. Thus,
He stands observantly behind
The sliding doors, today.

As a last expedient, he sits on
The dinner table and picks
Up a pen and paper, and
Freely writes what comes
To mind. Hours later, to his

Surprise, he is still writing
And poetry at that. Feeling
A bit more unknot, he
Divulges layer after layer of
The weight buried inside.

Panoramically, the young man
Sits inside a modest house,
Full of furniture and pictures
While the world spins outside.

He writes compulsively, in an
Eye-opening experience, an
Afflatus, to the helpless poet.

I

Descensus

Sat . . . On a baroque wooden
Chair, tattooed with renaissance
Imagery, inhaling life through
A dimly lit candle light.

Pretending to shine bright
At the desperate darkness
Transpiring through me, taking
Evil and transforming it on

Beautiful metamorphoses
Of emotional revelations.
Daring not to run, but

To sink in contemplation
At the unity of emerging
Inner sea and alien desert.

Last breath, close eyelids
Numbness
Silence.

Anima Mundi

II

Purificationis

Air flow . . . Suspended feeling
Fill with intoxication of blissful
Memories tainted by human
Experience, creator of empathy.

Opening eyes, accompanying sensations
Of absolute freedom, pulling burdens
Of a materialistic life, an empty life.

Grandiose revelation, one cannot
Live without suffering human
Conditions, for they are what
Makes us equal, one that is.

Darkness . . . echoing thoughts
Of parallel questions of which
Now seem obsolete; for a
Momentary purification of
Inner demons, whom once
Ran free, now throw their
Ashes to the wind, for another
Man or woman to feed.

Development

Dare to See

Amidst a foggy forest
Where no smell exists
Amongst the story, lays
A cave, dense, dark
And dysphoric to those
Who dare to see.

The cave in which
All is bury, gives rise
To many treasures to
Seek; for, what is
Death, grief and
Isolation to the
Poet, but instruments
Of illumination
Unbeknownst. Since
The sadder the story
The bigger the sonnet
Song; but like every

Exploration story
Danger lurks beyond.
For the treacherous
And tentative rock
Shelter hides many
Malicious seeds. In

The morning gives
You treasure and
At night let's all its
Monsters roam free.

A Momentary Lapse of Honesty

And there she was, reclining
Against the backdrop of a slowly
Decaying and yet fast impressing,
Picturesque byzantine edifice.
With a seemingly peculiar and
Forgotten expression she stares
At the momentary empty space

Laying in front of her eyes,
But which is yet so full of life
Itself, but as if someone had
Turned the lights off she sees
Nothing, nothing is there to see
For there is more inside, she
Momentarily screams; silently

Communicating with the outer
Spiritual sensations of the afternoon's
Mellow and peaceful atmosphere.
She no longer wants to be this
Way, she has found that each
Time she sits there silently
Calling on god with questions

Of empty promises and answers
Of silent response it eats at her
Every time, for every time she

Dies a bit, deep inside, and that's
When she wishes that perhaps she
Could grasp all of this learned
Malice and quietly purify it by
The ocean's banks as she once
Believe her soul to be like.

Then a passing wind blows and
Knocks at her consciousness
Which reminds her of that
World full of life right in front
Of her eyes. Such light, such
Beauty she thinks at last. Then
She gazes at cocoa as he wags
His tail at the now responsive

Owner as water falls on the earth
As a forceful yet truthful smile
Appears on her face, as she has
Memories of her smile as she has
Of her frown. She lies a little bit to
Herself as she now pets her ever loving
Companion as does almost everybody

Else nowadays. Where loneliness and
Solitude stem from a world where is
More important to communicate
Through a phone than is to

Interact with each other.
As she unfortunately does

With her friends over a
Fictitious world in which
She exterminates all of her
Real world insecurities.
And there she remains, back
To where she started, asking
To herself why has she turned

This way. And to you the reader
That is, but my question. Why
Has she turned out this way?
Since her eyes are those
Of many whom now walk
Our streets, a true reflection
Of many whom look themselves
At the mirror, but do not dare
To look at into themselves.

Muses

For a young poet's distress
By lingering voices of
Many a source, wisdom
Old. For many are the
Messages to consult. So,
I put ink to paper, for
Restless they become.

To create harmony is
A mission, to create
Chaos is, but a choice.
For a coin is our wisdom
Flipped at random choice.

Many are there choices
As colors for eyes to
Behold. For what is
Happiness if there is
No sadness in the mud.

Greater are my thoughts
The simpler they become,
For complexity is the
Reason of the double-edge
Sword. To live, grow, love
And flourish on times to

Come. To die, to be nothing

And be forgotten, time has

No remorse; yet, forever

Will my words be carved

In your mind and your soul.

Ensueño

Cathedral bells resonate through
The echoing walls of this
Colonial city. Is *El Dia de*
Los Muertos and those alive
Celebrate what destiny
Holds for them. Colorful

Masks of skeletal design
Adorn the crowded streets.
Red hibiscus match the
Color of her lips, as her
Brown hair tones with
Her olive skin. Her eyes
Try to connect with me.
I wonder what colors do
Orchids grow around here?

Rain smell advocates the
Passing of future sentiments.
What if I run and try to
Abandon my fate? Coward is
That whom thus behaves.
Afraid of coming storms,
Missing the bestowed in-between.

There is Life

For there is life in every
Soul, there is love in all.
Many are there hearts which
May surf through these voids.

Life is a tendency that
Resides in us all, but
Living life is a joy of
The fortunate souls, for

There is much to feel
When you have loved. To
The few whom have lived

But not loved, there may
Be a question to solve.
What is the meaning of it all?

Compassion, Love or Desire?

Most of me is love and
Desire, it becomes strong
And compassionate, but
It is also miraculous. Can

I be more into defying
That which I cannot Desire?
Time has come and gone,
But I still can grab it,

Feel it and try it. Love
Is more to me than what
Love has come to define

Me. Waiting for it to
Imply me that love is
What makes me survive it.

Joy

Maybe tomorrow, maybe
Today, what I have done
It would make me better man.
Although, I feel there is room to

Innovate. I hear music in
My ears, I feel music in
My chest. Joy that kills
Is what they say.

Inside there is more
Than what I can say. Life
Is beautiful, so I make
Sure that I comprehend,
Its meaning and what is
Not there, but I still feel that
There is much to confess.

Infatuation

Move across the lake
And I will build a brid-
Ge on it, move across
The ocean and I will

Flight above it, leave
For the stars or down
Underground and I will
Reach for them; but

Do not ever leave my
Heart for it will not
Mind, even if you tried,

What you have done for him.
Nor would it mind that
You have suffered for him

Two-way Mirror

As I lay here thinking
About my day, life has
Come through me in
The face of your beautiful

Self. Ha! Maybe there
Is missing a piece in my
Own self, maybe is just
Life being ironic in a
Way, or maybe is just
My imagination of what
Should be there, to complete

A part of myself. Feelings
Can be joyful, feelings
Can be hurtful, in many ways.

Expectation

Through the balcony of
Life I saw the feelings of
My life, for every corner of
My heart took possession of

My eyes. Was there ever
Such a desire at my hands
At ripping all the negative
Influences lying on my sight?

For my legs never felt so
Weary of walking without
A guide. It feels like I am

Barely breathing, breathing
At the starlight. Waiting
On the sunset's bright daylight

Fate

To the young man's desire
Which lie deeply at heart,
To be once none other than his
Imagination of what shall pass.

Life seems to trouble such
Frantic desires of that
Perfect life, for ironic
Seem the moments on

Which they do not come
To pass. This is the mystery
That storms my mind, for

It shows that these moments
Are the best ones so far.
Fate, unshakable power of life.

Leaving the Nest

Seeking water in a well,
The well which gives its
Water to me and that which
Keeps me from seeking the sea.
I wonder, if I were to quest
To the sea, would I travel
The world without stopping?
I would. I would be happy

In the sea, to travel and travel
With the sea under my feet.
I'd traveled beyond these eyes
Can see. No reason not to leave!

But, here is the well and it gives
Its water to me. Why then,
Should I venture to leave?

Anticipation

Sitting on the bench of an
Old railroad station my
Heart pounds at the rhythm
Of the tracks. Tons of emotions

Lay on my shivering heart,
For here approaches the
Haunting melody of the train's
Humming. All seems to be ending

At such a frightening pace,
But need not worry, I know
That tomorrow I will be waiting

For the same moment to pass.
More and more it will help me
To become that which I am not.

Peace of Mind

At the boat's edge, where the

Sunset's view seems ineffable,

Wave induced rhythmic

Movement emanates the

Conscious feeling of serenity

Confirmed by the peaceful

Incantation of the twilight's

Natural mystic.

Satisfy my soul (background song cries)

Nothing has so great a

Value, that with so little

We feel so important.

And I inhale my cigar laughing,

Laughing to the introspection of

Realizing the ignorance of many

At inhibiting the human

Excellence, absolute empathy

Yet a kindred soul hugs me

And reminds me that

We are not alone.

Satisfy my soul (background song cries)

Thoughts of a Citizen of Sybaris

On the thirtieth floor
Of a building, white cur-
Tains swing melodically
At the serenity of the
Night. For no reason

Or purpose I walked
Outside to watch. Me-
Mories overloaded my
Mind and a smile
Came to my mouth.

Lost with the feelings of
The moon high above, no
Thoughts came to mind.

Minutes that felt like hours,
Sensations greater than a
Lifetime of words. Wished
It would be like this forever,
And never speak a word.

Sentiment now gone forever,
Sentences are now calling
From the door. Long live
Our sensations and
Yield to nothing more.

The Promising Dream

Papier-mâché figurines
Compliment the outer
Window view. Feelings
Serenity from a well
Spent night. Outside
Is snowing, is snowing
Out in the park.

Blue eyes penetrate
Deep into my mind,
Hypnotizing away fears
And any doubts that might.
Her body rises and
I notice her long and
Orangey socks, in an
Otherwise naked body,
Her favorite, I reply.

As she gently glides to the
Seat of an overly vivid
Black piano, her hair
Reflects the depth of
The instrument's meaning.

Still in bed, her overly
Joyful and profound
Interpretation of an

Awfully familiar and
Yet strange classical
Composition shakes
My bones deep down.

Guitar in hand and
An unlikely modern
Hat on my head, are
Enough to corroborate
With her in such an
Important moment,
Our moment.

Woken up from a dream,
A dream more vivid
Than any reality ever played.
For years have been since I felt
Such love, such longing at
Surrendering my heart, my all to
A lover. Meaning of such dream,
I do not have, but what has the dream
Given me is a dream to follow, now.

Revealing Eyes

Those eyes, those blue eyes
Obscure like a cloud sky
Full of hidden light, gave
Me peace on the first sight.

Eternal was the second in
Which I shared a connection
So deep, with you inside.
Like the sound of a broken

Glass on the pavement, my
Heart exploded inside.
Emotions absent by time

Had found place once more
In a fainting lifetime.
Those eyes, those blue eyes.

Disillusionment

Initiation it seems, the
Mother of all things
Pleasurable; for everything
Conceivable, and once
Beautifully romanticize

Eventually leads to
Disillusionment and
Contempt. We suffer
Not because of things
In themselves, but
Because Of our judge-
Ment about them.

As the blind who follows
Pleasure, and the stoic who
Seeks intellectual suppression.

Acceptance

In a vine field, quietly resting
Under a shadow, pensive,
Waiting . . . an old man
Smokes his pipe. Nothing

Particularly interesting
About him, yet there is
Something to admire. A
Calmness, a tranquility of
Mind and composure
Which Rivals all
Extravagant exhibitionism.

A face forged by time, a
Canvas marked by
Countless emotions and
Experiences. Although, not
Appealing in detail, as
A whole, evokes feelings
Of wonder and contemplation
At the air of expectation,

Of a longing and acceptance
At what inevitably is yet to
Come. The eyes project a
Flourishing of a child like

Warmth with temperance
And an understanding.

Curiously, this I always
Remember when pondering
About things yet to past.
The angst of not kno-
Wing is thus replaced
By wonder and calm.

Pain

Pain, is like a black hole
That sucks the light from
Your universe. It marks
The passage of time, by
Slowing it due to the felt
Emotions. It accrues to

Extreme density and
Makes time inexorably
Strenuous. Like a hundred
Years of lessons are learned
In a few seconds, and

The further you succumb
Into its pressure, the harder
The pull and the more
Infinite seems its nature.

Reductio ad Absurdum

1st Proposition

What is like, the experience
Of death? Is it like that of
Profound darkness? Darkness
Forever, & never more light.
Or is it like having never existed?
Outside of time .What is it like
To sleep the slumber from
Which you never wake up?

Where you surrender your
Liability to those coming
Behind & you rest from
The inertia of everyday life.

2nd Proposition

What is like, waking up from
Never having gone to sleep?
Is it like having the experience
Of living from never having
Existed? As if from outside
Of time? Born as *Tabula rasa*

Our destiny is not. Minds
Renew, & thus we experience
Everything in a new light; a
Sense of wonder, & newfound
Excitement in everyday life.

∴

Is death the ultimate kindness?
Or is it a selfish act? Is it the necessity
For not being aware of the continuity
Of time? The forgetting of things renews
The Wonder & newfound excitement; it
Is the recharged battery that shines in
A new intensity & carries on the light.

Apology

The

Past,

Present,

Future,

My Apologies.

To the past for forgetting, it

Was necessary. To the present for the regret and

Vexation of your impending station, it is verily exacting; and

To the future, for the dissipation and demoralization of your prospects, it will be difficult, I am sorry.

The System

I

Am,

Love,

Belonging.

I am you, and

Humankind is our order.

You are me, and our safety is in

Numbers; so is our destruction if I beats WE, and WE is used till

Left unconscious. Heed your needs, and you will not be bent to your knees by the will or the deeds of others.

Time

Initial conditions, paramount. The
Inevitability of it, tantamount,
And selection is naught.
Thrown into the river, the
Space-time current of history,

Your coordinates, right now.
Should you choose to fight the
Current? Or should you drift in

The wave? The ripples of your
Actions extending forward and
Backward, molding the path; and
Laterally, affecting other paths.
The dynamic of the motions,

Driven by the causality of the
Apparent chaotic complex system,
Riddled with uncertainty, often

Leave you distraught; left with
The ineffability of time and
Consciousness so familiar to
Our minds. Time is consciousness,
Consciousness is the qualia of

Time. Time is the mesh

Of the tapestry of the uni-
Verse and consciousness

Is the knots. The river?
The initial consciousness that
Was released as if from
A dam (the Big Bang). Thus,
Fear not the fret of it, for

It'll all come out in the wash,
Crashing in the Elysian Fields,
When the chronology is to halt.

The Sublime

In the grand expanses of land, space and sea,

I see. The vastness with which they provide

You, allow for humility to creep. Compelled to

Confront your smallness, time seems to slow to

A beat. The unnerving awe with which they

Confide you, allow for the transgression of your

Ego to be. Since, the cacophony of the personal

Voices, drown your inspiration in a pit; quiet

Your mind, allow the polyphony of the spirit to

Speak. Only then, through your ego it will seep.

Curiosity

Let's confess, to the curiosity
Of the unknown. What is the
Aim of that yearning to discover,
What is just beyond? Why

Follow the intuition of thoughts
About things that cannot be
Thought of, only explored? Why
The necessity of the discovery?
Herein lays the paradox.

So then, let's hope that the pre-
Sumption, does not grow into a
Pandora's Box. For hell is paved
With good intentions, and it
Is easy to follow that road.

Imagination

Imagine a slow dance of dandelion
Seeds floating above a *fjord*. Also
Picture a Galleon down below.
Do you see it? Now the Wind as it
Caresses the mountains and your
Body, whole. Do you feel it? Can
You listen to the water? The ropes?
Where does all that come from?

Creativity

Why is it that we like to press
On to others whatever idea
Is formed? Which often
Expresses as the impulse to
Fulfill that particular vision
Invoked. How to manifest

It into a vivid formula is the
The only requisite involved.
From There you must surely
Obtain an experience of flow;
Which most likely executes
The originally intended goal.

Optics

Let, from the source, the
Object come into the light.
Where from obscurity the
Subject passes through the
Shadow into the bright.

There, a peacock appears
Fanned out on an endless
Patch of lawn. Where the
Eyes of the *cauda pavonis*
Absorb reflections from its

Many different frames of
Reference; and its fractal
Nature makes it, so that the
More it changes, the more it
Tends to remain as it was.

With its illumination grated
Through a prism, that gives rise
To a series of polychromatic
Encarnación. The light gives

The phenomenon of the visible
Spectrum, but it is not the limit
Of its scope. Rather, it is a
Small window, within the
Frame of much larger door.

Nostalgia

(Chopin's Ballade No.1 in G Minor plays in background)

Early morning, before the

Sun sets in. Getting ready

In front of the mirror,

Before the daily battle

Begins. A slow injection of

Compressed emotions, rushes in;

While bottled up memories of

Childhood, start to sneak within.

As fragments, at first, they

Begin. Later as stories that

Turn to folklore of the culture

With which you strongly i.d.

I remember. I remember!

The bay, the mountains and

Trees. The friends with which

I often fought on streets, and

Those which I, eye to eye did

Not meet. What times! What

Childhood! It feels like reveries.

What of this picture? Stuck

Between the wood and the mirror,

In which as a teenager, I keep.

Are you a stranger or is it really,

Dear old me? I no longer

Remember you really. What

Secrets you keep? I swear,

They are no longer in here, or

At least it seems that way to be.

Did I keep your promises, or did

I selfishly revised them while you

Were tucked away in your sleep?

Others too are now gone, and we no

Longer their histories script. Who

Conserves their diaries? Who cares

Of the legacy they leave? Hopefully

We converse with our children

Before it is our turn to decease.

Sanctuary

Where is your church?
The place in which you
Express yourself profoundly.
The palace of no inhibitions,
Just you and your most
Humility inducing questions.
The temple in which the
Conundrum of sincerity is
Lifted; where your feelings
Morph, lightened and your
Thoughts form with clarity.

Where is your prayer?
Among the common and
Vainglorious sections, or
In the humble and gregarious
Directions? Should you find
That your actions usually
Follow the current social
Dictations, maybe is time
To go alone and face your
Inexorable isolation. Although,

Given often to vacillation,
Why should you stop with
Your perjurious indiscretions!
No one seems to care for

Your transgressions. So then,
Why don't you visit with
Yourself and engage in
Some serious conversation.
Would you dare to enter
A house built on such
Unsteady foundations?

Where do you shelter?
When the world's white
Noise volume is not enough
To drown out the desolation.
You could continue down
Into the pursue of seductive
And precocious pleasures, but
Does it suffices to go along
Without any other intention?

Further and further, until
No room is left with air
And you agonize by slow
Suffocation. What then,
Would you do with your
Disowned denomination?
Knowing that not one
Person can relieve you of
The struggle and tribulation.

Allegory

We must begin with the
Allegory of the marionette.
Since, it serves as a true
Reflection in the form of
A vignette. Supported by
The strings of attachment

And the cross bar up, above
The head. Man is born free,
Or so they say. For the
Attachments that sustain us,
Easily become our restrains.

When they gradually transform
From safety buckles into
Restraining belts. Often though,
Through the stages they propel
Us, but eventually they tend to
Immobilize us in the play.

These chains, anchored by
The direction of the passion,
Guides our hand to act in almost
Every way. The shackles which
Secure the precision of our

Movements, allow for confident
And ardent displays, but can
Also turn to contracts that
Tighten to contrition and swell
The pain. Therefore, we usually
Avoid those attachments to

Brake, and from the fear of
Further constraints, we refrain.
Hiding behind the equilibrium
Extended by the acceptance
Of the limits of the threads;

And wearing costumes that
Serve as reminders of what
One should expect. So, do not
Downplay the importance of
Your freedom, be brave, brake
Free of the yoke given at birth.

Go ahead, do it, move beyond
The boundaries set. Command
Your body, be the master of
Your faith. Don't be hesitant of
What's next. Come on! Do . . . it.

The Frontier

Once I wandered to the
Edge of my imagination.
In wonder of what may
Be beyond what's expe-
Rienced and its impre-
Ssions. To go deeper and

Travel farther than the
Learned conceptions and
Collect the rewards for
The labor, no matter the
Felt trepidation. There,

A great wall appeared,
Brownish red in its
Coloration. The wall
Where all knowledge
Appears to evanescent
Behind the surface, is
Filled with engravings of

Primitive and geometric
Origin, which seem to
Have been since its
Inception, interlaid. The

Terracotta partition of the
Horizon of reason and the
Border of the primordial
Mind, Ylem; and the key
To entering this kingdom
Is the *caduceus* with the
Ouroboros lemniscate.

Simulation

Now we discover, that the
Actions of the future affect
The past and that the past
Actions affect the future;
And that they are one, and
The same one. Thus it seems,
That the present is nothing,
But the experience of the finite
Within the infinity, bound.

The denial of visions of the
Future and the memories from
The past, together with the
Experience of the ever-present
Consciousness, are the necessities
Required at the start. There
Is nothing more exciting and
Sensuous than the stimulation of
The mysterious and the unknown.

As when you discover something
Which you had never experienced
And you live it for the first time.
That bit of anxiety and ambiguity,
That at first scares you, but then
Releases wondrous sensations and
Keeps you alive. Therefore, the

Prime reason for existence, is the

Freedom to continually explore

And develop this newly formed, I;

And the constant expansion of

Mind. Interconnecting loops of

Vibration at particular resonant

Patterns, each forming a section of

An ever expanding spiral, in time.

Information

It is all about the information.
Who or what carries it, and in
Which dimensions. To be logged
In the timeframe allotted and
Continually ask questions.

With each timeline medium
Influencing the knowledge that
Is attainable. Giving rise to new
And unique properties which are
Dispersed within each generation
The information is received,

The data is transformed and
Ultimately released as nourishment.
Where, sometimes its fruits are
Ripe, but seldom rotten; never stale
Just not yet allowed to flourish.

We Are Actors and All the World's a Stage

The stage is set, the
Curtain rises. We are
Ready to begin. Thus the
Actor comes forward and
A beam of light hits his
Face. An introduction to
The stage is made, follow-
Ed by the development
And ultimately his death.

The curtain falls, the
Play is complete. We
Are ready to begin. Like
An actor, a lead role is
Ours to take, no other
Is given, for the others
Are for others to take.

We thus play to the best
Of our abilities, until
It is done once again.
Like a script in a movie
We are lead for a path
To undertake; infinite-
Simal improvisations, but
One screenplay to partake.

The chaos of individual
Drama, unmagnified by
The macrocosm interplay.
Each time we revisit
The story, the more
There is to comprehend.

Although torn asunder
By the anxiety of sonder,
Fear not your role to play.

Eulogy

If I die today and you buried
Me tomorrow, would heaven cry
And earth thrive on another
Tormented summer? Would

It be an eloquent and divine
Story, or a sad song of sorrow
And folly; for the saddest of
All the stories, is the never ending

One. As that of the sad lovers
Whom most beautiful of stories
Is always doomed to fail and die.

For is never a one sided story
That of love and glory, since
Both are different paths of life.

Recapitulation

III

Crucis Supplicium

This is it, this is the end.

The end of the descent.

No more word play, simile, metaphors or intellectual trickery. The

Phantoms of the ultimate chimera no longer accommodate the

Forbidden intuition. A life of seeking, to an end of silence.

Do I take the wager

Or accept the vacuum?

Do I reject to the question

Or accept what follows?

Hence, the silence.

The Taboo of the

Forbidden Intuition,

The Sanbenito Coronation

Of our collective superego.

Ex Hoc Mundo
ad Animam

Epilogue

Lay to rest, has been carried
The young bard. A brave soul,
Whose explorations, cleansed
Many obscure aberrations from
The young man's mind. The late

Bard was no wordsmith, he
Was no philologist; simply he
Was a poet at heart. A conduit
Of the deepest, most sincere
Emotions, any young man can have.

A mystery, he lives in paper, for
No longer is the young man able
To recognize him. He is close
To him as another person could.

An analogy, a comparison of his
Mannerism and expressions to
His. A superficial level of sym-
Pathy, of anguish and relief.

Yet, the young bard's explorations
Mean more to him, that he could
Presently understand. Like a drug,

The words felt like an explosion,
An apprehension of things just not
Yet understood, but somehow, someway

Wonted; as if they had always been
There. A castaway oasis, crafted by
By conventional ought, and ought nots.

What then? What is to happen from here?
Is it the end of young man as well as
The poet? The poet is dead, but
It is not the end of the artist.

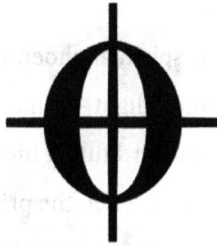

IV

Resurrectionem

Orchestral voices filled with
Organ melodies, resurrect
My soul from the ashes.
From darkness to light,
Recomposing the organism

Of the spiritual phoenix to
A restored flight. Permeating
Is the bird full of life,
For it has broken the prison
Clinging to his mortal life.

www.ingramcontent.com/pod-product-compliance
Lightning Source LLC
Chambersburg PA
CBHW050555280326
41933CB00011B/1853